May your heart and paws
embrace responsibility, just
like Polly!

Denise McCormick

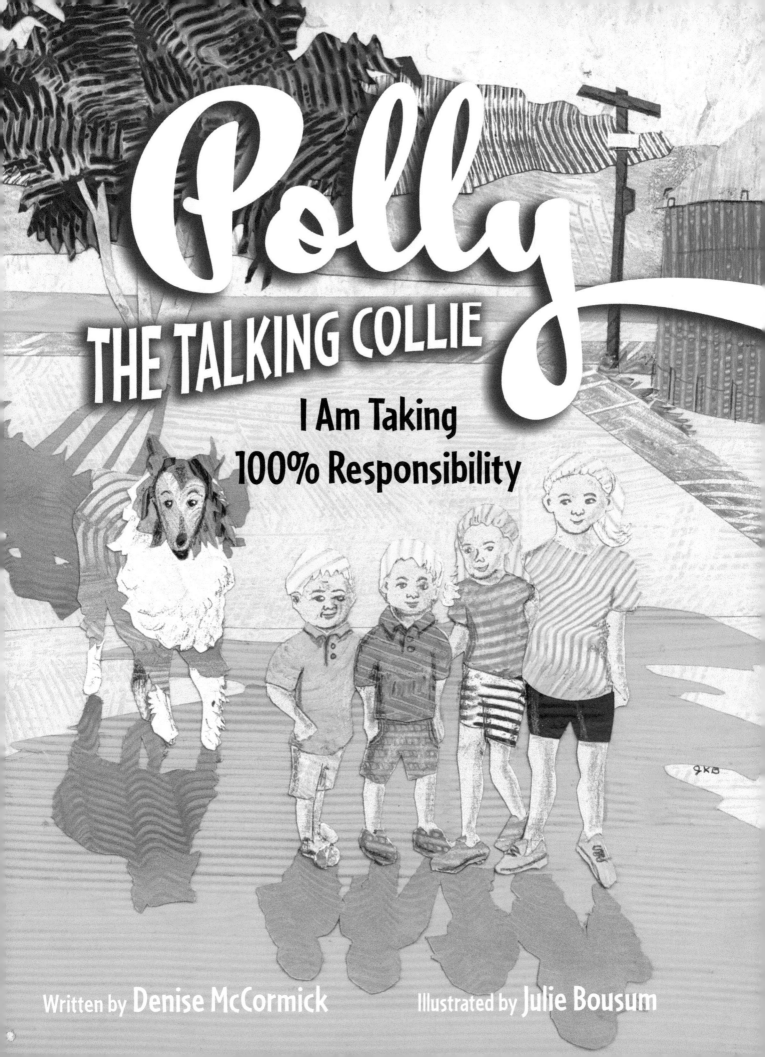

This book is dedicated to my husband, John, for his constant support during the last 48 years. He has always been an example that if you care about family, friends, and farming the land, you can achieve incredible success through hard work, patience, persistence, and perseverance.

Thank you, John, for consistently taking 100% responsibility for Mac Farms Inc.

I don't remember the day very well.
I was just a puppy when my new
parents came to take me to their
Iowa farm.
We drove along a gravel road to their
big, white farmhouse surrounded by
corn and bean fields.

Mom and Dad put me inside an enormous fenced-in area in their yard to protect me. It had a doghouse, water, feeding bowls, and lots of toys. I love to romp in the huge yard and ride in the back of the four-wheeler they use for yard work and checking the fields.

7

8

After a few weeks, it was time to learn how to stay safe while running in the three acres surrounding our farmhouse. My parents gave me a special collar and put an invisible fence around the whole yard.
I was trained where the boundaries for this fence are, and I was free to run and play as long as I stayed on the inside of the invisible fence. This meant that I wouldn't get hit by a car.

I had a game I played when a car or truck came up the road. I ran alongside my invisible fence to see if I could outrun the vehicle. It was so much fun! Also, all my barking let my Mom and Dad know someone was in our area. Barking to protect the farm was one of my responsibilities.

My name is Polly, and everyone calls me Polly the talking Collie. That's because my barking always gets their attention.

As a puppy growing up, I had so many life lessons to learn and so many responsibilities on the farm. At first, I didn't understand what responsibility meant. Responsibility means taking care of my jobs and duties. Taking one hundred percent responsibility means I did what needed to be done, and I took ownership of my actions.

One day a groundhog made the mistake of venturing into my yard. I said to myself, "Stay focused, Polly!" This is my territory, and I won't let any intruders come into my yard without being invited by Mom and Dad.

I decided to show that groundhog who was boss. I barked and chased him up a small tree. Since groundhogs are not known for their climbing abilities, he fell, and I chased him out of the yard. I pranced proudly back to the house and told Mom and Dad what I had done.

"Good girl, Polly!" Dad said. He hugged me and gave me a treat.

My big responsibility was
helping the farmers.

Planting corn and beans on
our Iowa farm was so exciting!
When the big machinery arrived,
it was my responsibility to let
everyone know they were outside.
I greeted the workers with
enthusiasm and a happy attitude.

First, we prepared the soil by plowing and tilling to make it ready for the seeds. Then a really big planter with a gigantic tractor pulling it drove into the field and began planting corn and beans.

They grew all summer and needed lots of water, sunlight, and nutrients to sprout and start growing into tall plants.

It wasn't all work all day long. This was another life lesson that I learned. Play is good! Sometimes Dad said, "Polly, let's go for a ride."

I was quick to jump in his truck. Oh, how I loved to go for coffee! When he went inside, I moved to the driver's seat and pretended I was driving away. Why were people inside the coffee shop laughing at me? I was a good driver!

As we drove home, I hung my head out the window. I loved the feeling of the wind in my face and seeing the world zoom by. It was good to delight in the simple things!

Then it was back to work. Dad and I drove around and checked the fields to see how the crops were doing.

23

One day, something
special happened.
I finally met the grandchildren and all
the cousins at a family reunion!

"Woof! Woof!" I talked to them.
"Welcome to my Iowa farm!
I'm so happy to see you!"

"Kids, meet Polly the talking Collie,"
Dad said to our grandchildren.

We played games of fetch and ran all
around the farm. We enjoyed being
outdoors together! I often had to help
find lost toys and comfort a child who
was crying. I loved lending a paw to
help! I watched them very closely and
made sure they stayed safe as they
explored and played.

After the farmers took care of
the crops all summer, it was time
for the harvest.

Then I got to see a huge combine
and grain buggy pulled by a giant
tractor. They drove around the field to
harvest the crops and stored them in
enormous grain bins until it was sold.

It was busy, and I loved running up
and down the yard as the machinery
and semis took the crops out.

Years and years went by.

Now that Dad is retired,
I have taken on a new role.
When I was a puppy, Dad helped me
learn how to take responsibility on
the farm. Now he is free to learn from
me. I've taught him to accept treats,
play, and enjoy the simple things.
We explore and then take plenty of
rests together. We are loyal, and we
don't hold grudges.

I'm an old doggy now, and I have a new responsibility.

I am a service dog.

I stay by my farmer's side every day and love him unconditionally.

31

About the Author

Denise McCormick has a lifelong background of memorable farming experiences, having lived six years as a child on the farm where her great grandfather started Kennedy's Dairy in the late 1800s.

When she married John 48 years ago, she moved to their fourth generation Heritage and Century farm where they live today.

Denise attended Iowa State University and graduated from Iowa Wesleyan University with her Bachelor's in Education. She went on to receive her Master's in Education from Viterbo University adding a K-12 Reading Specialist and K-8 Reading Endorsement. Denise taught at the University and graduate school level for 10 years as the Education Lecturer, Reading Specialist and Iowa Writing Project instructor.

Denise received a Literacy Award from the State of Iowa for demonstrated contributions to language development and learning of literacy from the Iowa Council of Teachers of English Language Arts.

Denise redirected and is a Certified Jack Canfield Success Principles Trainer in his Methodology, now coaching educators. Denise recently returned from Ghana, West Africa, as she focuses on her commitment to Links Across Borders which builds libraries in Ghana.

The I AM series of children's books is written to help students understand The Success Principles™ and to develop a growth mindset.

You can find fun activities, resources, and additional information about the farm on her website **www.denisemccormick.com**.

Denise lives with her husband John on their fourth generation farm in Mt. Pleasant, Iowa. They have two daughters and five grandchildren. She enjoys reading, writing, traveling, and spending time with their grandchildren and their dog Polly.

About the Illustrator

Julie Bousum lives in Iowa with her husband, Curt, with whom she has three wonderful children. Julie attended Iowa State University to earn both her bachelor's degree in Art Education and later her graduate degree in Educational Leadership. Julie taught secondary visual arts and language arts classes for 45 years and has taught in college classes and summer camps.

As someone who spent her childhood on her grandparents' farms, Julie found the opportunity to illustrate a book about Denise and John's farm and special friend Polly to be an honor. In addition to creating artwork, Julie enjoys singing, gardening, and most of all, watching her eight grandchildren participate in their activities!

Printed in the USA
CPSIA information can be obtained
at www.ICGtesting.com
LVHW071642090824
787811LV00012B/96